Developing Reader titles are ideal for children who are confidently using their phonics knowledge ar ̶ ̶ ̶read short, simple sentences with only a little help. Frequently fluency and confidence.

Special features:

Short, simple s

Frequent repetition of main story words and phrases

George sees the glasses and puts them on.

They look funny on George!

"Oh, George," says Peppa.

She takes the glasses off George.

"Here you go, Pedro," she says.

Careful match between story and pictures

Large, clear type

"Take a look at this chart for me," says Mr Pony.

Peppa looks.

"Now look at this chart," says Mr Pony.

Peppa says what she can see on the charts.

Ladybird

Educational Consultants: Geraldine Taylor and James Clements
Book Banding Consultant: Kate Ruttle

LADYBIRD BOOKS
UK | USA | Canada | Ireland | Australia
India | New Zealand | South Africa

Ladybird Books is part of the Penguin Random House group of companies
whose addresses can be found at global.penguinrandomhouse.com.

www.penguin.co.uk   www.puffin.co.uk   www.ladybird.co.uk

Text adapted from *Peppa Pig: Peppa's First Glasses* first published by Ladybird Books Ltd 2013
Read It Yourself edition first published by Ladybird Books Ltd 2019
This edition published 2024
001

Printed in China

The authorized representative in the EEA is Penguin Random House Ireland,
Morrison Chambers, 32 Nassau Street, Dublin D02 YH68

A CIP catalogue record for this book is available from the British Library

ISBN: 978-0-241-56540-7

All correspondence to:
Ladybird Books
Penguin Random House Children's
One Embassy Gardens, 8 Viaduct Gardens, London SW11 7BW

Peppa's First Glasses

Text adapted by Ellen Philpott

Peppa and George are with
Pedro Pony.

They are jumping in
muddy puddles.

Splash! Splash!

Pedro is jumping in
a muddy puddle. Splash!

"Oh! My glasses have
come off!" says Pedro.

Now he can't see very well.

Peppa and George look
for the glasses.

George sees the glasses
and puts them on.

They look funny
on George!

"Oh, George," says Peppa.

She takes the glasses
off George.

"Here you go, Pedro,"
she says.

"Why do you have glasses, Pedro?" says Peppa.

"My daddy says I need
them," says Pedro.
"He is an optician.
Opticians test your eyes."

Pedro gives Peppa an
eye test.

"Close this eye for me,"
says Pedro. "What can
you see?"

"I can see George,"
says Peppa.

"Now close both your
eyes," says Pedro.
"What can you see?"

"I can't see at all!"
says Peppa.

"You need glasses,"
says Pedro.

"Mummy, I need glasses,"
says Peppa.

"Why?" says Mummy Pig.

"If I close both my eyes,
I can't see!" says Peppa.

"No one can see with
both eyes closed!"
says Mummy Pig.

Peppa wants to go
to the optician.

Pedro's daddy gives her
an eye test. She puts on
some funny glasses.

"Hooray!" says Peppa.

"Take a look at this chart
for me," says Mr Pony.

Peppa looks.

"Now look at this chart," says Mr Pony.

Peppa says what she can see on the charts.

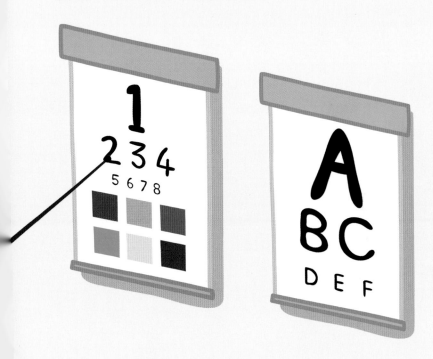

Peppa looks at all
the glasses.

"Come here, Mummy,"
says Peppa. "Look at these!"

Some of the glasses
look very funny!

"I like these glasses,"
says Peppa.

Mummy Pig likes them.

But Mr Pony says Peppa
can see very well. "No need
for glasses!" he says.

"But I want glasses!"
says Peppa.

"I do have some sunglasses,
if you like," says Mr Pony.

Peppa looks at the sunglasses.

"Hooray!" says Peppa.
"I like my glasses!"

How much do you remember about the story of *Peppa Pig: Peppa's First Glasses*? Answer these questions and find out!

- Who finds Pedro's glasses?

- What do opticians do?

- Why can Peppa not see anything when Pedro tests her eyes?

- What does Peppa get from the optician?